Top Tips for

D0537698

Over 300 Top Tips and Handy Hints

for Canoeists and Kayakers

Loel Collins and Franco Ferrero

Pesda Press - Wales

www.pesdapress.com

Published in Great Britain 2005

by Pesda Press
'Elidir'
Ffordd Llanllechid
Rachub
Bangor
Gwynedd
LL57 3EE

ISBN   0-9547061-4-5

Printed in Great Britain by

Cambrian Printers - Wales

Introduction

After the phenomenal success of 'Top Tips for Coaches' we decided that there was a need for this book. The top tips come from our combined experiences in kayak and canoe, on salt and fresh water, around the world. Experience is often hard won, and ours was gained at home in the UK and abroad in places such as the European Alps, Scandinavia, Canada, the USA, Peru, New Guinea, Pakistan, Iran, Nepal, Costa Rica, the Seychelles and Zambia.

The book is designed to be browsed and the distilled experience it contains to be thought provoking. We hope you enjoy it.

If you would like to contribute top tips to future editions, please contact us by e-mail at info@pesdapress.com.

Photos

Front cover: Dino Heald

Back cover: Left - Franco Ferrero, Middle - Helen Metcalfe,
Right - Ray Goodwin.

Top Tips for Boaters

1. Rules are for the guidance of the wise... and the blind obedience of fools.

2. Remember: PMA... Positive Mental Attitude.

3. Be flexible... there is always a plan B.

4.   Practise 'entryism'. If you don't like the system, get
        in it to change it.

5. Kayaking is a whole body sport.

6. Consciously use your feet more. Transfer the power through the footrest when forward paddling and use your feet to push the bow in the direction you want to go when turning.

7. Look after your feet. Get good footwear designed for water use.

8. Chunky footwear often won't fit in modern river boats and wetsuit bootees don't offer enough protection on stony ground. One answer is to take the insoles out of a pair of walking boots and put them in your wetsuit bootees.

9. In winter, use a pair that are half a size too big and wear woollen socks. Toasty!

Top Tips for Boaters

10. Never paddle anything blind.

11. Time spent in reconnaissance is never wasted.
     (Military maxim). Make that seldom.

12. Once you have assessed the hazards, chosen a line, and decided to run it, forget the hazards and focus on where you need to be.

13. If you think about the hazard... that's exactly where you'll end up.

14. "Never put your body where your mind hasn't been first." (Quote from a test pilot).

Top Tips for Boaters

15. Before running a tricky section, imagine running the section, doing all the moves and finishing it with a big smile on your face. If you can't visualise a successful outcome... don't do it!

16. Visualisation is a skill. Skills need practice. So use the techniques on easier sections, often.

17. On a long journey the last mile or so often seems the hardest because your body starts shutting down too early. Con yourself into believing you've still got 5 miles to go and the last mile will feel much easier.

18. Funny how surf waves get bigger when the sun goes behind a cloud and smaller when it comes back out again.

19. Measure surf the way 'boardies' do. They only measure the part of a wave that you actually surf on, so you have to knock a bit off the top and the bottom. That way when the surf forecast says 4 foot and clean you'll know what to expect and you won't wet yourself looking up at a wave that you would have described as 7 foot high.

20. When estimating surf wave height, do it standing up on the beach. They look a lot bigger when you are sitting down in your kayak.

21. Learn surf etiquette, 'dropping in' is a sure way to get yourself a good kicking.

22. Read 'Kayak Surfing' by Bill Mattos.

23. Keep out of the way of boardies. Kayakers have the forward speed to catch most waves while boardies may have to wait ages for the 'right wave'. Why piss them off?

24. Be strong, and be true to yourself. Paddle that difficult rapid or that choppy sea because you want to, not because you are afraid of losing face.

25. If you have decided not to run a stretch of water and one of your friends runs it successfully should you change your mind? If his or her run made you realise that the line is easier than you thought and within your ability, by all means. But don't run it because your friend got away with it.

26. If the people you paddle with would give you a hard time for choosing not to paddle a stretch of water... ask yourself if you really want to be with them anyway.

27. If you find that you are the only one carrying any safety and rescue gear, ask yourself if you really want to paddle with those guys.

Top Tips for Boaters

28. Train hard, fight easy. (Airborne forces maxim).

29. Play hard, boat easy. (Boaters maxim).

30. Be cool... or get mad! Find what works for you.

31. The more skilful a paddler you are, the safer you are. So train hard.

32. On the other hand, to quote William Neally: "It's better to be lucky than good."

33. You can't depend on luck.

34. Read 'Kayak' by William (not Bill) Neally. It's a blast.

35. Skill is the 'rubber' in the system. When the river levels rise or the sea state worsens despite the forecast, having a reserve of skill makes the difference between being terrified and having a more exciting time than you had in mind.

36. If the first time you put a skill under pressure is in a survival situation, you might not be able to 'cut the mustard'... then what?

37. Find places to practise and play where the technical difficulties are high but the consequences are low.

38. Develop a 'bomb-proof' roll. It's a lot more comfortable than that long cold swim through the surf.

39.   Develop a 'bomb-proof' roll. It's a lot safer than swimming in white water.

40.   Develop a 'bomb-proof' roll. It's quicker, safer and warmer than any of the other options a sea kayaker has.

41.   Develop a 'bomb-proof' roll. Think of your 'cred'!

42. Until you have a 'bomb-proof' roll, practise three rolls on each side every time you go paddling.

43. If you haven't reached that stage yet, read 'Kayak Rolling' by Loel Collins.

44. Play and surf! It's fun... and all those unintentional capsizes will help you develop a 'bomb-proof' roll.

45. Your paddles should provide you with feedback... so get a good, strong but lightweight pair.

46. You can't get feedback from a scaffolding pole!

47. Buy the best paddles you can afford. People will lend you a good boat... nobody will lend you their best paddles.

48. Unless you have very big hands, beware thick paddle shafts. It's a good way to develop the wrist injury tenosynovitis.

49. Don't use a 90° feather, another way to develop wrist injuries, go for 70° or less.

50. Wearing gloves has the same effect as thickening the paddle shaft. If you suffer from cold hands, buy a pair of 'palmless mitts'. Your hands stay warm and your skin is still in direct contact with the paddle shaft.

51.   If you are travelling abroad use paddlelock™ splits.
      That way you can stash them in your boat.

52.   If the water was serious enough to break or lose
      your paddles, your spares had better be as good
      as your normal paddles.

53. Relax your grip on your paddles. You'll get a better top arm extension, avoid wrist injuries and get less tired.

54. Relax your grip even if you paddle in rough water, trust me... nobody ever needs to be told when to tighten their grip.

55. Basic principles: Keep your paddle as upright as possible when you need the power, and as horizontal as possible when you need support or are using a turning stroke.

56. Even on the sea, forward paddle efficiently with an upright paddle. As the wind increases in strength and your paddle start to 'flutter', lower your paddle just enough to stop it happening.

Top Tips for Boaters

57.   If you see a 'squall line', lower your paddles before the wind hits you.

58.   If it's really bad go for a stern rudder and run downwind or low brace to windward.

59.   Keep one blade in the water as much as possible, no point letting the wind catch both blades.

60. In rough water of any type, keep a blade in the water as much as possible, either paddling, steering or bracing. The paddle will provide you with feedback and help dampen movements that might otherwise lead to instability.

61. In an open canoe, keep the (single) blade in the water all of the time. Slice it through the water to change its position.

62. Never use an 'air-brace'(paddle held horizontally in the air above paddler's head). It doesn't work, it makes matters worse by raising your centre of gravity, and above all... it's not cool!

63. Braces work best when they are at right angles to your boat and in contact with the water.

64. If you are in a narrow slot you'll have to make do with a 'stern brace' unless you want to end up with your paddles wedged across the slot. Ah... the art of compromise.

65. Low brace when you see it coming (prevention), high brace when you didn't see it coming (reaction) and the boat is too far over for you to be able to use a low brace.

66. High or low brace, keep your elbows bent and your muscles flexible if you would rather not experience a shoulder dislocation.

67. Relax! If your muscles are tense the slightest movements are transmitted right through your body, making you tippier.

68. Think of your abdominal muscles as a shock absorber.

69. Smile! It's really hard to be tense when you are smiling.

70. If you paddle on the rough stuff get a good helmet. No, not a 'cut down' fashion statement, a real helmet.

71.   Carry some 'gaffer tape'. You can repair boats, clothing, tents... you name it. I've even used it for a temporary repair on the neck seal of a dry-cag!

72.   Gaffer tape is also one of the most useful bits of first aid equipment you can have.

73. Chewing gum makes a great 'caulking material' for sealing small holes or the gaps around an improvised bung or plug.

74. Cable-ties are great for improvising links on backrests or footrests.

Top Tips for Boaters

75. Carry a lighter, there is no finer way to warm up and improve morale than standing around a driftwood fire on a wild beach.

76. Rubber fetishists wearing wetsuits, beware of standing too close and having 'melt-down'.

77. Don't leave your socks too close to the fire.

78. Light your fire below the highest High Water mark so that the next big tide will remove all traces.

79.   Don't waste your time with rope for tying boats on roof-racks. Get yourself some self-locking straps.

80.   For the inevitable time when you forget them and have to improvise with a throw line, learn how to tie a 'Lorryman's Hitch'.

81. If you paddle tandem, talk to each other! It's all about communication.

82. If you are running a rapid in the front of a tandem open boat, look over your shoulder now and then to make sure that your partner is still there!

83. Don't mess with the locals! Especially abroad where you are unfamiliar with local customs.

84. It always pays to be friendly and polite.

85. Find out about local customs before travelling abroad. In some countries something we wouldn't even notice, such as walking around with bare arms and legs, can cause great offence.

86.   "When in Rome…"

87.   When travelling in an unfamiliar country, avoid
      talking about religion or politics.

88.   Try and learn a bit of the local language. Even a
      few sentences from a phrase book shows willing
      and ensures a better welcome.

89. Never offer anyone a bribe. It's too risky.

90. If needs must, the trick is to look shifty and wait for them to make the offer.

91.   Never get separated from your boats. Stay/keep up with the porters or mule/donkey/camel/elephant drivers, no matter how fast or slow they go.

92.   Never trust any mode of transport that has a mind of its own.

93. If you are travelling into a wilderness area bear in mind that the bush pilots have a saying: "Any landing you walk away from is a good one"!

94. You can fit seventeen-foot boats in a Twin Otter aeroplane.

95. On committing multi-day trips, if you need to consider bank protection you should probably portage.

96. As a general rule, be wary of paddling anywhere where you are not at the top of the food chain.

97. The clue about wild animals is in the name. Give them plenty of room... they're wild!

98. Walk noisily in bear country.

99. Bear repellant is sprayed (as a last resort) AT THE BEAR! It's not like mosquito repellent!

Top Tips for Boaters

100. In the wilds you are either a threat or food for the local wildlife, Know how not to behave like either!

101. Bear cubs are cute, cuddly and always have a mum who isn't!

102. Bloody Moose, Bloody Moose, Bloody Moose!

103. When paddling on big volume rivers, go down the big wave trains, they are usually much easier to handle than the boily areas in what might appear as a 'sneak line'.

104. If you are in a boily area of water sit upright and relax.

105. Try and wait till the rapid has lost some power before breaking out (USA - eddy-in). The eddies at the top of a big volume rapid are often boiling seething monsters.

106. If you have to break out (eddy-in) into a big boily eddy, go as fast as you can, keep your hull flat, lean back and plane across the boil line.

107. When breaking out (eddy-in) in technical water, use plenty of edge.

108. When running technical rapids, break them down and work from safe platform to safe platform (eddy to eddy).

109. Take the time to read the water.

110. Use the water as much as possible.

111. When packing a white water kayak for a multi-day trip, put as much as you can in front of the footrest, even if it is only cans of tuna.

112. Good advice found in an old 1950s campcraft book: "After your first camping trip make 3 lists. The things you used every day, the things you used occasionally and the things you never used. The next time you go camping throw out everything from the last two lists."

113. When packing an open canoe use a couple of large dry bags. It makes life easier when lashing them into the boat or when portaging.

114. When packing a sea kayak, use several small dry bags rather than a couple of huge ones. It makes it easier to fit things through hatches.

115. Carry a large, lightweight kit bag. If you have to camp more than a few metres from your sea kayak you can load all your little dry sacks into it.

116. When preparing for a sea trip, imagine that you are going to have to carry all that kit on your back, and reduce it to a minimum. That way you'll spend less time packing and unpacking your boat and more time enjoying the scenery.

117. Always carry your boats well above the high water mark. You'll sleep much better that way.

118. Empty boats can be blown away in high winds. If the overnight forecast is poor and you have to leave the boats on an exposed beach, partially fill the cockpit of the windward boat with sand and lash all the boats together.

119. Don't leave the navigation to the leader. Keep track. What if you get separated or the leader is taken ill?

120. When crossing to an island, time it around slack water (make the midway point slack water), it makes all your tidal calculations simple, the tides cancel each other out!

121. Read 'Sea Kayak Navigation' by Franco Ferrero.

122. You have a moral responsibility to be able to help your friends. Practise rescue techniques.

123. While you're at it get yourself on a first aid course.

124. If you are a white water boater, get yourself on a WW Safety and Rescue course.

125. In bright conditions, wear eye protection in the form of sunglasses and peaked hats, especially on the sea.

126. Sun block is essential.

127. Try and avoid paddling on/in polluted water!

128. Avoid paddling in built up areas on the first flood after a long dry spell. All the muck accumulated in the storm drains and sewers gets flushed out.

129. If you must paddle on polluted water, avoid eating and drinking until after you have showered and changed.

130. If you must eat or drink, use some of your drinking water to rinse your face and hands first.

131. If you need pulleys to recover a kayak, you are probably pulling in the wrong direction.

132. If you've wrapped an open canoe, you may well need pulleys!

133. Prevention is better than cure.

134. When setting up bank protection, try not to rely on one system. Have some form of back up.

Top Tips for Boaters

135. In any kind of water, don't make physical contact with a swimmer until they have calmed down.

136. Panic is misdirected energy. If a swimmer won't calm down try to lure them towards safety. Make sure your boat is just far enough away that they can't actually catch you.

137. Chase boating is a risky business. Ask yourself if you have the skill to cope. Would you be of more use running down the bank with a throw line?

138. Read 'White Water Safety and Rescue' by Franco Ferrero.

139. When paddling in 'bandit country' (i.e. where fishermen object to people paddling), change before you get to the river.

140. Use a shuttle bunny or buck to avoid having to leave your car at the side of the river.

141. If you must park by the river, consider taking the roof-rack off and leaving it in the boot of the car out of sight.

142. Leave a copy of 'Trout and Salmon' in plain sight on the rear shelf of your car.

143. Paddle well within your limit so that you can paddle most things on sight, scout from your boat and keep bank inspections to a minimum.

144. Never leave the shuttle car keys in the car that is at the start point of the trip.

145. Never put the shuttle keys (with electronic immobiliser) in your buoyancy aid pocket.

146. Whatever signals you use, make sure that everyone in your group is using the same ones!

147. Use one-handed signals, you'll probably need the other one for hanging on.

148. Keep signals simple and obvious.

149. Confirm that you have received and understood a signal by repeating it back to the sender.

150. Always point in the direction of safety, the route the person should paddle. Never point at the hazard, the route the person should avoid.

151. If you are only interested in forward speed, the only points of contact you want are the seat and footrest. Go for maximum freedom for the body to rotate.

152. For playboating and hard white water you need to transfer power in 3 dimensions. Go for maximum body contact with the boat: deep seat, tight hip pads, backrest, padded thigh braces.

153. Sea kayakers spend a lot of time forward paddling but need to deal with the rough stuff as well. It's a compromise: comfortable seat, footrest, backrest and hip pads... but not too tight.

154. When travelling upwind, keep looking over your shoulder. You won't hear that trawler till it's almost on top of you.

155. Keep a 'weather eye' on open water. Look upwind and in the direction the clouds are travelling from. That way you won't be caught by surprise.

156. If you don't know much about weather, look for signs of change.

157. Dark clouds moving fast are usually bad news.

158. A dark line travelling over the water indicates a gust of strong wind or even a longer-lasting squall.

159. A white line travelling over the water is a severe squall.

160. Keeping a weather eye is sound practice but don't forget to get a weather forecast before you set out!

161. To encourage better use of your body when paddling, imagine a ball held in place, between the paddle loom and the front of the buoyancy aid.

162. Alternatively imagine your arms, paddle and body form a box shape which should be maintained when paddling.

163. Develop an understanding of your body's movement and actions within the boat.

164. Remember, balance and speed are related.

165. Even when you stop moving the river hasn't.

166. In moving water think 'Spangle'. (Speed and Angle).

167. Spend time developing co-ordinated movements as part of your warm-up.

168. Warm up and stretch physically and mentally prior to a hard run!

169. Spend time ensuring the equipment, all of it, is the correct size for you.

170. With the wrong kit you will be fighting your equipment and not paddling.

171. Make sure your boat's padding fits you and DOES NOT constrict you.

172. Use paddle wax in the paddle shaft to reduce the need to over-grip the paddle. It will improve your subtle blade control.

173. Subtle blade control comes from the hand closest to the blade in the water, i.e. use both hands to control the paddle.

174. When you are playing, try not to do the same thing more than four times in a row.

175. Never be afraid of going back to the foundation skills, these form the basis of all effective paddling.

176. Most paddlers' problems are due to poor posture. Poor posture prevents rotation which prevents effective strokes.

Top Tips for Boaters

177. Spend time in other kinds of 'canoe'. If you kayak paddle a canoe for a while, if you canoe paddle a kayak for a while! If you do both try a ski!

178. Invest in some good coaching.

179. £30 airbags will save your £700 boat.

180. True experts have a broad foundation of skills. Try lots of different things.

181. Play with purpose. If you have a target or outcome (however trivial) in mind, you can compare your performance.

182. Is your roll failing at the end of the stroke? Try cocking your wrist of the upper hand towards the shoulder at the end of the sweep.

183. Is your roll failing because your body is coming up early? Nod your head towards the paddle blade that's in the water as you come up.

184. Is your roll failing because the head comes up early? Look at the surface of the water as you roll up.

185. When practising rolling, avoid over-extension of the upper arm by putting a tennis ball in the upper armpit and try to keep it there during the roll.

186. On a river rescue remember: paddler, boat, paddles, in that order.

187. In open water: boat, paddler, paddle, in that order.

188. Clean rope: no knots, use hitches, you don't need a handle in your end, be dynamic.

189. "There is no try. Only do or do not. If you try you will fail" - Yoda.

190. Duct tape: have lots.

191. Electricians tape: have lots!

192. There is a difference between river right (right facing downstream) and wave right (right as you ride the wave – facing upstream). Know it.

193. You can't shout across a river, SO DON'T EVEN TRY.

194. Always carry a throw line.

195. If you carry a throw line you have to carry a knife.

196. Be careful with that knife... you could have somebody's eye out with that thing.

197. You should be able to get your knife out, and in the case of folding knives open it, one handed.

198. A boater's knife is a safety tool, it can be small and discreet.

199. In most places you can't justify carrying a knife once you are off the river (a legal requirement in the UK). So leave it in your buoyancy aid pocket.

200. The best way to ensure you don't forget your knife when you go boating is to leave it in your buoyancy aid!

Top Tips for Boaters

201. Bent-shaft canoe paddles need to be about 4cm shorter than your straight paddle.

202. When choosing a canoe pack put durability (including the buckles and fittings) before comfort.

203. Always pick a canoe pack with a waist belt and tump line.

204. Learn to tie quick release knots or only use hitches.

205. The difference between being good and being an expert is detail!

206. The difference between an expert and a jedi is ego!

207. The old boys know how to do it as well, listen to old farts!

208. Don't buy any canoe you need help to carry.

209. When travelling with your boat make sure you can carry your luggage and boat in one go.

Top Tips for Boaters

210. Sit on the seat with your feet tucked under, you don't have to kneel!

211. Set the seat at a slope towards the front to help.

212. Make your luxury good thick socks on a canoe trip.

213. Don't let your paddling buddy burn them because they are so 'minging' he thinks you've thrown them away.

214. Get on the level with the river. Rapids look much larger when viewed from above.

215. When paddling tandem, odd numbers work on the portage. One, three or five packs are better than two or four. (You have a boat to move as well!)

216. If you don't know the portage, carry your gear over the portage and familiarise yourself with the route. Then bring the canoe.

217. If you know the portage move the canoe first so you can put your packs straight into the boat, save picking them up again!

218. Help each other picking up a large pack.

219. Two or three canoe lengths offshore may be the safest place to be in a lightning storm.

220. When map reading, the larger the contour interval, the less you can tell about the river.

221. The closed or 'vee' end of a contour line always points upstream.

222. Where contour lines cross or run very close together, you'll find an abrupt drop - a falls or canyon.

223. No point taking a map if you haven't learnt to map read.

224. Don't pack all your emergency signalling equipment in one canoe.

225. Tag barbed wire fences with brightly coloured surveying tape so other canoeists won't run into them.

226. Check for dew on the bottom of your boat before you head off to sleep. If the bottom's wet, you can bet there is no rain in sight.

227. Remember weather top tips never really work.

228. Pick up the tempo; don't just pull harder for power.

229. Cleanly slice the paddle blade into the water, then firmly 'anchor' it before you pull.

230. When applying the power keep the paddle shaft as vertical as possible when you stroke.

231. Use your torso, not your biceps, to move the boat.

232. Sometimes the only answer IS to pull harder!

233. The river is heading downhill fast enough – only paddle down river if you need even more speed.

234. When using signals, always indicate the line to take, not the hazard.

Top Tips for Boaters

235. Surf wax on your seat gets your bum to stick to the seat.

236. Surf wax on the cockpit rim gets your spraydeck to stick.

237. Surf wax on your loom get your hands to stick.

238. In flat-hulled boats it is sometimes good to fit a sitting block to raise the paddler, this really helps performance.

239. To help with breaking out, dropping the inside shoulder forwards into the eddy helps drop the edge and trim the boat forwards.

Top Tips for Boaters

240. Breaking in is 'edge', breaking out is 'lean'. (it's all to do with speed).

241. In a canoe it is rarely ever 'lean', it's usually 'edge' achieved by shifting weight over a knee. (It's a speed thing).

242. Paddling is a case where the whole action is greater than the sum of its component parts.

243. Paddle with water in the river.

244. If you carry all your kit in one large bag to help on the portage, try putting your kit in smaller coloured dry bags inside. It's dryer, more secure and the colours help you know what to open up.

245. If you make lots of late finishes try different textured bags as well.

246. Get your ears checked.

247. Try before you buy.

Top Tips for Boaters

248. When travelling further afield remember a length of 6mm climbing cord. On buses, horses, even helicopters, you'll want it for tying your boat on.

249. Breaking out is NOT a sign of weakness.

250. On a trip, stay dry, stay warm, keep fed and watered and get plenty of sleep.

251. At some point you will just have to go boating!

252. If you take it with you know how to use it.

253. Learn CPR.

254. Practise your CPR before you need to use it.

255. Pray you never have to use it.

256. Without plenty of water the body will not work, drink lots!

257. If you boat in a dry suit go to the loo before you get in your boat!

258. Gentlemen! Invest in a relief zip for your drysuit... it's worth every penny.

259. The beauty of the canoe is its versatility.

260. Stretch your back out after a long day on the water, before you pick up your boat!

261. The trick to paddling the canoe is to be prepared to move about.

262. In a canoe the trim is important, put something in the boat that rolls around so you can see how trim works.

263. Grading is irrelevant, it's about you and if you want to do it or not.

264. There are only three grades: easy, hard and harder than you're prepared to paddle.

265. If you wear glasses tie them on!

266. To be honest, the only way to develop your skills is to go boating.

267. Going overnight? Consider a tarp - it's smaller and lighter than a tent.

268. Lots of small dry bags are better than one large one.

269. If you get seasick easily, dress to stay cool rather than warm, it helps.

270. When looking for a campsite on a river, start mid-afternoon and take one early rather than late!

271. If it's not going well get off the water and come back another day!

272. Don't do it for photos!

273. If you are carrying splits, have good quality splits.

274. When doing trips, consider taking splits in your luggage rather than a full set of paddles on the plane!

275. Go Alpine, light, fast and safe.

276. When travelling on local buses watch out for sharp edges on locally made roof-racks!

277. When portaging in the jungle and having to cut a path, use a machete in one hand and stick in the other and have your mates stand well back. You'll save fingers, avoid bites and win friends.

278. At altitude, 3000m+, altitude illnesses are a potential problem. The big range rivers present problems on the river and the trek in!

279. At least once, try boating to music!

280. Outfitting your kayak is best done with minicell foam, contact adhesive, sandpaper and time. Manufactures kits don't cut it!

281. It might be new school where you live but it's probably old hat somewhere else!

282. If in doubt portage.

283. There are only two types of weir. They are either a piece of cake... or they kill you. (See previous top tip).

284. Before your fly-drive boating trip remember to specify a roof-rack on your hire car.

285. Don't be worried if you forget; some wood and cable ties can normally improvise pretty well.

286. If you have to improvise, take a set of felt tip pens!

287. Return your hire car in the dark!

288. Look after your back, warm it up, stretch it out and be careful.

289. On a trip good footwear is important, wetsuit boots don't cut it!

290. Look where you want to be next.

Top Tips for Boaters

291. When looking at a rapid, let the water do the work for you if you can.

292. On a big water day remember not to open your doors if your car gets stuck in flood water.

293. Only boat if you're fit and well.

294. The difference between a 2 river and 3 river day is the shuttle. Get them sorted!

Top Tips for Boaters

295. Everybody swims!

296. A bad day on the river is better than a good day in
the office.

297. Only pick fights with rapids you can win! WHEN YOU PICK THE WRONG FIGHT TAKE YOUR BEATING LIKE A MAN (or at least try to).

298. When you paddle out beyond the reef, bear in mind that the route back is often hard to spot from the ocean. Have a clear mark on land or fix your point with a resection or transit, otherwise getting back in will be painful and often bloody!

Top Tips for Boaters

299. Life as a river bum is short lived, learn a trade!

300. Sponsorship is a two-way thing, sponsors forget it but so do 'sponees'.

301. Hey... It's only boating!

302. Safety is the state of your mind NOT the state of your equipment.

303. Paddle in time with the sun, not your watch.

304. Insects and animals become more active when the world about you is changing. Listen, look, feel the bites and change your plans accordingly.

Top Tips for Boaters

305. If the water levels are rising and you keep asking yourself whether you should get off the water... you probably should.

306. Then again... one of my best river runs happened when I ignored the advice and managed to pull it off!

307. One of my worst was when I ignored that advice and didn't pull it off.

308. We all make mistakes, the trick is to learn from them.

309. Boating is a soul thing, we all do it for the buzz, we just have different buzzes.

310. Enjoy your boating.

Top Tips for Boaters

Notes

Notes

Also available from Pesda Press

For more details of these and many others, visit our online catalogue at

www.pesdapress.com